ARTISTS' OXFORD

Cliff Bayly Jane Carpanini John Doyle
Dennis Flanders Ken Howard Ken Messer
William Matthison Hubert Pragnell
Dennis Roxby Bott

Text by
MALCOLM HORTON

Contemporary Watercolours

For Eleanor, Josie, Lewis and Sam

First published in Great Britain in 2005 by

CONTEMPORARY WATERCOLOURS LIMITED
165 Parrock Street
Gravesend
Kent DA12 1ER
Tel: 01474 535922
Website: www.contemporarywatercolours.co.uk

Set in Garamond. Artwork by Janet Davie. Project co-ordinator: Susan Grant

Printed by Oriental Press Limited, UAE
Scanning by Max Communications Ltd., Sidcup, Kent
Pre-press finishing by Quantock Studio, Sidcup, Kent

ISBN 09526480-3-2

Front cover: ***All Souls - John Doyle***
Back Cover: ***A View from Hinksey Hill - Ken Messer***

CONTENTS

INTRODUCTION

In 2001 Contemporary Watercolours published "Oxford Watercolours" followed, in 2004, by a companion volume, "Cambridge Watercolours".

They were an attempt to produce a contemporary version of Rudolph Ackermann's mighty tomes of the early nineteenth century entitled "History of the University of Oxford: Its Colleges, Halls and Public Buildings" and its Cambridge companion. These publications were lavishly illustrated by four distinguished topographical artists, Pugin, Mackenzie, Nash and Westall, and undoubtedly raised the profile of topographical watercolour painting which, as a result, became a unique English genre.

Both of the twenty-first century books were based on paintings which had been produced for specific arts alumni projects with the individual Oxbridge Colleges over a period of fifteen years.

The Oxford book is now out of print and it was suggested that we reprint. We have, however, much material that has been produced since 2001 and also it was felt that the interest and scope could be widened, to include more general Oxford views and use additional artists, who are associated with Oxford such as Ken Messer and William Matthison.

Matthison comes from the bygone Edwardian era and illustrates perfectly the appeal that Oxford has always had for eminent artists over the centuries, including J. M. W. Turner. We have included two views which are unusual and, in some ways, unique. The view of the Oxford skyline from the Radcliffe Observatory and the Degree Ceremony in the Sheldonian.

As well as thanking all the contemporary artists for their valuable contribution I would like to thank the Executor of the William Matthison Estate, Rowland Cooper, for supplying valuable source material. Thanks are also due to Julian Blackwell for permission to reproduce the painting on page 19. Finally, I would like to thank the Heads of House and Fellows of the Oxford colleges for their support and co-operation in producing many of the paintings which appear in this book.

Malcolm Horton
Gravesend, Kent.

Cliff Bayly, R.W.S.

Born in London and trained at St. Martin's and Camberwell Schools of Art, Cliff Bayly was elected a Fellow of the Royal Watercolour Society in 1984. He was, for twenty years, Head of Graphic Design Degree Courses at Maidstone College of Art.

He has exhibited regularly at the Royal Academy Summer Exhibition and Bankside Gallery, home of the Royal Watercolour Society. He has been a winner of the prestigious annual Singer Friedlander/Sunday Times National Watercolour competition.

He now lives in Australia but returns to Britain for several months each year.

Jane Carpanini, R.W.S., R.W.A.

Jane was born in Bedfordshire in 1949 and was elected to the Royal Watercolour Society in 1978, establishing a reputation for expansively composed and meticulous watercolours. She was trained at Brighton College of Art and the University of Reading.

Her work is in the collections of the National Library and National Museum of Wales. She is also a member of the Royal West of England Academy and the Royal Cambrian Academy, and exhibits regularly within these societies. She has served as the Vice President and Honorary Treasurer of the Royal Watercolours Society.

In 1983 she was the winner of the prestigious Hunting Groups Prize, for the Watercolour of the Year by a British Artist.

John Doyle, M.B.E., P.P.R.W.S.

Born in Dulwich, London, in 1928 John is a past President of the Royal Watercolour Society and has had many exhibitions in major galleries in London and Canterbury Cathedral. A book, entitled "An Artists Journey Down the Thames", was published in 1989.

He has recently undertaken a peripatetic journey retracing and painting in St. Augustine's footsteps from Rome to Canterbury to celebrate, in 1997, the fourteenth hundredth anniversary of this famous event. This culminated in an exhibition at Canterbury Cathedral of the 300 or so paintings made in he course of the journey.

John now lives on the edge of Romney Marsh in Kent and readily acknowledges the help and encouragement he received in the early years from the distinguished painter John Ward.

Dennis Flanders, R.W.S., R.B.A.

Born in London in 1915 Dennis was unquestionably one of the greatest pencil and watercolour artists of the twentieth century. He attended evening classes in antique drawing at the Regents Street Polytechnic whilst working for a firm of fashionable interior decorators. He painted the scenery and architecture of the British Isles for over sixty years before his death in 1994.

He has been called the "Canaletto of our time" by Peterborough in the 'Daily Telegraph' and was, for some years, a graphic reporter with the 'Illustrated London News' and his pictures of London during the Blitz are treasures of the Guildhall Library and the Imperial War Museum.

A Freeman of the City of London, he was a member of the Art Workers Guild and served as Master in 1975. Two previous books have been published containing the body of his lifetimes work, "Britannia" in 1984 and "Watercolours in Academe" in 1995.

Ken Howard, R.A., R.W.S., R.W.A.

Ken was born in London in 1932 and is a member of the Royal Academy and Royal Watercolour Society. He was, until recently, President of the New English Arts Club, that bastion of figurative painting and drawing. He was official war artist in Northern Ireland in 1973 and 1978.

Since his National Service in the Royal Marines 1953-55 he has had a close association with the British Army, undertaking special commissions for them throughout the world, including portraits of the Royal Family. Ken's work is held in public collections including the Imperial War Museum, Ulster Museum, National Army Museum and the Guildhall Art Gallery.

He has studios in London and Cornwall and two books on his life and works have been published entitled "The Paintings of Ken Howard" in 1992 and "Ken Howard A Personal View" in 1998.

William Matthison

Born in Harborn near Birmingham in 1853 William Matthison was the quintessential Edwardian artist. He attended King Edward's Grammer School Birmingham and entered the Central School of Art in 1869.

He married Mary Fessey in 1878 and moved to Banbury in 1883 and then to Oxford in 1902. There he met Robert Peel, who was just beginning to break into the new and thriving postcard industry. Matthison became his principal artist. He produced over 70 views of Oxford and their scope was extended to include Cambridge, Devon, Cornwall, London and the Lake District.

He was a member of The Clarendon Art Fellowship and was Vice President of The Oxford Art Society for many years until his death in 1926.

Ken Messer

Born in Newport, Monmouthshire, in 1931, he was educated in the City of Oxford School. On leaving school he initially went into the prosaic science of accountancy, leaving after six years for a flying career with BOAC. This was cut short by a motoring accident and he then moved closer to his natural bent by entering the publishing industry. He eventually became Studio Manager in charge of Art and Design at Permagon Press.

At the age of 43 he left publishing to freelance as a graphic designer, which acted as a spur to his already burgeoning interest in watercolour painting.

He has since won three consecutive prizes in the prestigious Saunders Artist in Watercolour International competitions. His work has been published in five books and his work regularly appears at the annual open exhibition of The Royal Institute of Painters in Watercolours at the Mall Galleries.

Hubert Pragnell

Born in London in 1942, he studied Fine art at Goldsmith's college London and at The Ruskin School of Drawing and Fine Art in Oxford. He also has a degree in history from the University of Kent. For many years he taught history of art at an independent school in Kent (The King's School, Canterbury) and is now a tutor in History of Art at the University of Oxford Department of Continuing Education and attached to Kellogg College.

He has a particular love of landscape and architectural subjects for which he has received numerous commissions. He has been painting and drawing Oxford's rich architectural heritage since the 1960's. He has exhibited widely and his work has been sold abroad. Works have been reproduced as prints for a number of bodies including the former Royal Naval College at Greenwich, and Contemporary Watercolours.

He has also written and illustrated a number of books on British architecture. He lives in Canterbury where its cathedral is a constant source of artistic inspiration.

Dennis Roxby Bott, R.W.S.

Born in Chingford, Essex, in 1948, he attended the prestigious Norwich School of Art where he studied fine art painting and obtained a Dip.A.D. (Fine Art). He was elected to the Royal Watercolour Society in 1981.

Dennis, who now lives in Sussex, has had regular one man exhibitions in London and Sussex notably Ebury Street Galleries, SW1, Worthing Art Gallery and Museum, Lannards Gallery Billingshurst and the Ogle Galleries.

He is a regular exhibitor at the annual spring and autumn Royal Watercolour Society exhibitions at the Bankside Gallery and in 1992 he was a prize-winner at the annual Discerning Eye Exhibition at The Mall Gallery in London. His commissions include the Wardroom of H.M. Royal Yacht Britannia, Sotheby's, American Express and the National Trust.

Malcolm Horton, author and publisher

Malcolm Horton was articled to a City of London firm of chartered accountants and qualified in 1966. He spent twenty years in industry and commerce with companies such as Beck and Politzer, Esso Petroleum and BOC International. The latter part of this period was spent in the printing industry, where he was, successively, chief executive of Williams Lea, and of international fine art printers, Westerham Press. In 1986 he set up an accountancy practice as well as a fine-art publishing business, Contemporary Watercolours. The watercolour business has not only allowed him to work with some of Britain's most talented watercolour painters but his peregrinations have given him an intimate knowledge of the beautiful towns and cities of the British Isles, particularly Cambridge and Oxford. In his spare time Malcolm Horton was, in the 1970s, a borough councillor for the London Borough of Bexley, and in 1983 stood (unsuccessfully) for the SDP in the General Election. His previous books, *Watercolours in Academe, Oxford Watercolours and Cambridge Watercolours* were published between 1995 and 2004. His hobbies include playing squash and watching Charlton Athletic F.C. He is married and lives with his wife, Valerie, on the Chart Hills, just outside Ashford in Kent.

The View from the Radcliffe Observatory by Hubert Pragnell

A unique opportunity

In the course of completing a view of Green College's Radcliffe Observatory, the college authorities granted access to the gallery at the top of the observatory. The view was magnificent and quite unlike any other in terms of the buildings encompassed. It has rarely been portrayed from this vantage point. One can only remember Frederick McKenzie's engraving in Ackermann's Guide of 1814.

It was, therefore, a great honour when the college allowed Hubert Pragnell access to this unique vantage point. The painting he produced is stunning and contains so many Oxford Landlmarks. It was felt appropriate, therefore, to include this view with an index, as a pictorial introduction to Oxford.

1. Magdalen College
2. New College
3. All Soul's College
4. New Bodleian Library
5. School's Quadrangle, Tower of the Five Orders
6. Clarendon Building
7. Sheldonian Theatre
8. Radcliffe Camera
9. Old Ashmolean (now Museum of History of Science)
10. St. Mary the Virgin
11. Trinity College Chapel
12. Exeter College Chapel
13. Merton College Chapel
14. Exeter College, Broad Street Block
15. Balliol College Hall
16. Balliol College Gatehouse
17. All Saints' (now Lincoln College Library)
18. Christ Church Cathedral
19. Ashmolean Museum
20. Randolph Hotel
21. Christ Church, Tom Tower
22. St. Mary Magdalen
23. Rewley House
24. Somerville College, Bldg
25. Oxford University Registry
26. St. John's College
27. Judges Lodging
28. St. John's College, Garden Quadrangle
29. St. Aloysius Roman Catholic Church
30. St. Giles
31. Radcliffe Infirmary
32. Somerville College
33. Radcliffe Infirmary
34. Somerville College Chapel

Hubert Pragnell 2005

ALL SOULS COLLEGE

Great Quadrangle by John Doyle

Hawksmoor's masterpiece

All Souls is one of Oxford's true anomalies having, neither graduate nor undergraduate pupils, only Fellows and post-graduate research workers. It was founded by Henry Chichele, Archbishop of Canterbury, in 1438 to commemorate the dead of the Hundred Year War with France.

The view depicted by John Doyle is similar to the one included in Ackermann's famous "History of the University of Oxford, its Colleges, Halls and Public Buildings", published in 1814. It is taken from the Radcliffe Camera, looking eastwards across Nicholas Hawksmoor's Great Quadrangle constructed between 1716 and 1734. He was a scholar and domestic clerk to Sir Christopher Wren who was, himself, a Fellow and Bursar at All Souls. Hawksmoor's twin towers, holding centre stage in the painting, are one of Oxford's landmarks and one of its *dreaming spires.* Clearly seen to the left are the bell-tower and chapel of New College and to the right, the cupola of Queen's and Magdalen's famous tower.

ALL SOULS COLLEGE

Codrington Library by John Doyle

Treasure from the Caribbean

The old library of All Souls, dating from the college's foundation in 1438, reflected the college's academic interests Theology, Law and Medicine. By the early 1700s, however, the old library was filled to capacity and it was indeed fortuitous and timely that Christopher Codrington, in 1710, made a bequest of £10,000 for the building of a new library.

Christopher Codrington (1668-1710) was the son of a wealthy plantation owner and Governor General of the Leeward Islands. He was a graduate of Christ Church and was a Fellow of All Souls from 1690 until 1697. During this time he turned to the profession of arms and campaigned in the West Indies and Flanders. In 1699 the soldier-poet-scholar succeeded to his father's estates and to his position as Governor General of the Leeward Islands. After early military and naval success against the French he failed in the Guadeloupe campaign of 1703 and was removed from public office.

Thereafter, Codrington concentrated his energies on theological and philosophical studies and amassing a huge library. After his death in 1710, as well as an endowment of £10,000, All Souls received his library of over 12,000 volumes. Codrington College in Barbados was also created from a bequest made by him.

The architect, Nicholas Hawksmoor, was in the process of putting together designs for the Great Quadrangle at All Souls at the time of Christopher Codrington's death. He rapidly revised his plans to incorporate an extensive new library along the northern boundary of the College site. The 200 foot long room of the library was completed in 1720 and was the first ground floor academic library in England.

John Doyle had long wanted to paint the Codrington Library and in 1995 he gained the permission of the college authorities to spend many weeks dwelling on this magnificent subject; surely the most impressive college library in Oxford.

BALLIOL COLLEGE

Front Quad by John Doyle

British Prime Minister and Chancellor of Oxford University

The catastrophe which was the First World War 1914-1918 had a seminal and deeply felt effect on not only the University but also on Britain as a whole. Things would never be the same again and the old order of class and privilege was to change forever. Over 14,000 Oxford men went to that bloody conflict of whom 2,700 died. Amongst those who survived was future British Prime Minister, Harold Macmillan (1894-1987).

Macmillan, who entered Balliol in 1912 had his studies interrupted in 1914 when he went to serve King and Country and wounded three times. The suffering and deprivation he witnessed both in the war and later in the Great Depression of 1930 was to have a profound effect upon him and defined his political credo. Later, in 1957, he was the first Conservative prime minister to serve as a one-nation Tory. He retired somewhat prematurely in 1963 due to ill health. He was Chancellor of Oxford University from 1960 until his death in 1986, and was the first serving British Prime Minister to hold this office.

Another one-nation Conservative Prime Minister was Edward Heath 1970-1974, also a Balliol man who had seen action in the Second World War (1939-1945).

It is an interesting fact that since the Second World War until the beginning of 2005 there have been eleven British Prime Ministers, eight of whom were educated at Oxford. In chronological order they were

1945-51	Clement Atlee	(University College)
1955-57	Anthony Eden	(Christ Church College)
1957-63	Harold Macmillan	(Balliol College)
1963-64	Alexander Douglas Hume	(Christ Church College)
1964-70	Harold Wilson	(Jesus College)
1970-74	Edward Heath	(Balliol College)
1974-76	Harold Wilson	(Jesus College)
1979-90	Margaret Thatcher	(Somerville College)
1997 -	Tony Blair	(St. John's College)

BLACKWELLS

No. 50 Broad Street by Ken Messer

An Oxford Institution in four generations

To commemorate their 125th anniversary Blackwells commissioned local artist, Ken Messer, to produce a poignant view of their main bookshop, number 50 Broad Street, where the company was founded in 1879. Its founder was Benjamin Harry Blackwell and his heirs, three generations later, are still running the business which remains a private company with over fifty retail book-shops worldwide.

In the beginning Blackwells dealt, almost exclusively, in second-hand books. The business expanded and leases of surrounding properties acquired and by the turn of the century its lists included new books. Fiction, children's books, reference works and foreign books were comprehensively covered.

The need for more space in Broad Street culminated, after consultation with Trinity College, in the construction of an enormous underground terraced chamber below the south-east corner of Trinity. This room of 10,000 square feet and with three miles of shelving, found a place in the Guinness Book of Records for having the largest display of books for sale in one room anywhere in the world. Known as the Norrington Room it was named after Sir Arthur Norrington who was the President of Trinity at the time and, founder of the Norrington Table of inter-collegiate finals results.

In Ken Messer's painting there are shown the usual well-known features which grace this part of Oxford, its heart ,so to the speak, such as the Sheldonian Theatre and Clarendon Building and also the Indian Institute Building. This can be seen beyond the Clarendon on the corner of Holywell Street and Catte Street. It was constructed in 1885 in 18th century English Palladian-style, to the designs of Basil Champneys. It was founded following a proposal by Sir Monier-Williams Boden, Professor of Sanskrit for the purpose of spreading knowledge of India amongst Europeans and, conversely, where Indians could learn about the West. Controversially, in 1968, the building was appropriated by the University for use as offices. It now houses the History Faculty library. The legacy of the Indian Institute, however, is preserved in the form of its museum, transferred to the Ashmolean and its library transferred to the New Bodleian, where it remains the most extensive open-shelf library on India in Europe.

BLACKWELLS

BOARS HILL

View from Hinksey Hill by Ken Messer

Oxford's dreaming spires

Boars Hill which is situated three miles to the south of the city centre has been a source of inspiration to poets and painters alike. It was, however, the poet Matthew Arnold (1822-1888) who first made the area famous with his poems "The Scholar Gypsy" and "Thyrsis". Matthew Arnold Field was bought by the Oxford Preservation Trust in 1928. It was from here that he saw "*that sweet city with her dreaming spires*" a line which he immortalized in the poem "Thyrsis", written in 1861.

Other poets inspired by the dreaming spires and who lived on Boars Hill include John Masefield, Robert Graves, Robert Bridges and Edmund Blunden. However, Boars Hill's most enduring resident in terms of visual legacy was Sir Arthur Evans, the eminent archaeologist, whose Jarm Mound overlooks Oxford. This 50 foot high artificial hill contains at its summit a view indicator covering Oxford and the surrounding countryside.

Ken Messer follows a long line of distinguished artists to paint a view of Oxford's dreaming spires. The usual vantage point for such a view is Boars Hill but, Ken decided to paint his view a little lower down from Hinksey Hill. The trees in the foreground give an enchanting rural feeling to the painting without being too obtrusive. A feat that can only be achieved in the spring.

BRASENOSE COLLEGE

Radcliffe Square Front by William Matthison

Morse and the case of the brazen nose knocker

Brasenose was founded in 1509 on the site of several mediaeval halls, the most notable being Brasenose Hall, from which the college acquired not only it name but eventually the famous bronze sanctuary knocker or "brazen nose". The original knocker was taken to Stamford in 1334 by the master and scholars who were themselves seeking sanctuary from the continual rioting between town and gown, which characterized Oxford in the 13th and 14th centuries. Edward II did not approve of the setting up of a rival seat of learning in Stamford, so forced the dissident scholars back to Oxford, but the bronze knocker did not return until much later.

In Colin Dexter's Inspector Morse books, the fictional Lonsdale College is frequently featured. From the authors precise geographical references Brasenose is obviously the model. In fact, in the "Carlton" Television screenplays which produced thirty-three episodes between 1987 and 2000, Brasenose was featured in seven episodes. This is perhaps not surprising since the locations advisor for the series was Dr. Phillip Gasser, the real life Bursar of Brasenose at the time. Like the author, in Hitchcock style, Dr. Gasser appears in each episode.

It is not generally realized that Colin Dexter is a Cambridge man, having graduated from Christ's in 1953. A final irony, however, is that the famous "brazen nose" knocker did not return from Stamford House until 1890, when the college bought the house to regain possession of the original knocker. Stamford House was then part of Stamford School where Colin Dexter was a pupil.

To day the original "brazen nose" knocker has pride of place in the Hall hanging over High Table. A replica from 1509 is to be found on the main gate.

CARFAX

The High's West End by William Matthison

A tale of three city churches

This view was painted in 1905 and shows by contrast to the grave academic buildings, the western end of "The High", wearing the aspect of an ordinary commercial town. Flourishing business premises, protected from the sun by colourful awnings, a horse drawn tram and a bit of the old Mitre Hotel at the right hand end, all encapsulate Edwardian Oxford.

At the far western end of the The High stands the ancient tower of St. Martin's Carfax, formerly the city church and the centre of municipal life. Carfax is the place where the four roads from the North, South, East and West Gates of the city met. It was the highest point of the old city. The name is derived from the Latin *quadrifurcus* (four-forked).

St. Martins was originally granted by King Canute, to the Benedictine monks of Abingdon in 1034. The church to which the tower belonged was demolished in 1896, in order that the road could be widened. The benefice passed to All Saints which became the city church until 1971, when it was Converted into Lincoln College's Library. The livings then passed to St. Michael's at the Northgate in Cornmarket, which is now the city church.

The old church tower of St. Martin's Carfax has now become officially a Clock Tower and Civic Belfry. The clock dates from the 17th century as do the original quarter boys (figures of men holding clubs) whose 1898 replicas strike the bells every quarter hour. (The original quarter boys are in the Museum of Oxford).

Opposite the Carfax, on a corner, now occupied by the Abbey National, is the site of the Swindlestock Tavern, opened in 1250 and closed in 1709. This was the tavern where the infamous riot of 1355 broke out, between Town and Gown. It lasted for three days and scores of citizens and students were killed, ostensibly over an argument concerning the quality of the tavern's wine! It would seem that the Nation's drink problem goes back a long way.

CHRIST CHURCH COLLEGE

Peckwater Quad by Dennis Roxby Bott

Dean Aldrich - A man of many parts

The Peckwater Quad was designed by the Dean of Christ Church, Henry Aldrich (1647-1710), and completed in 1714. Aldrich was a man of many parts, theologian, talented musician and above all a skilled amateur architect. He is also thought to have designed the Queen's College library and All Saints Church, High Street. He was also the University Vice Chancellor from 1692 to 1695.

As a result of James II's folly in appointing as Dean a Catholic, John Massey in 1685, admissions fell and so did James, in 1688. An Anglican, Henry Aldrich, was appointed Dean in 1689 and admissions rapidly increased so that more accommodation was needed. The former Peckwater Inn site was reconstructed between 1705-1714 to form a most elegant and homogeneous three sided, Classical quad with nine staircases - The Library was added in 1772 to complete the fourth side of the Quad. The quadrangle, although named
after a mediaeval Oxford family who gifted the site, is a great tribute to Dean Aldrich, who is reckoned to be Christ Church's most industrious and convivial Dean.

In Dennis Roxby Bott's painting the gap between the buildings leads into the Canterbury Quad, constructed by James Wyatt in 1783, with its great Doric gateway leading out onto Oriel Square. It replaced the buildings of the former Benedictine Canterbury College (1362) which was acquired by Christ Church at the time of the Dissolution (1542).

CHRIST CHURCH COLLEGE

Tom Quad by Dennis Roxby Bott

Two Princes, one in love with Alice

During the Civil War Charles I used Oxford as his military base. He set up his Court at Christ Church in 1642 and lived in the Deanery for four years, until his surrender to Oliver Cromwell. Christ Church has acted as a magnet for aristocrats ever since.

Two of Queen Victoria's sons, the eldest (the future Edward VII) and the youngest, Leopold, matriculated at Christ Church. Edward stayed for two years from 1859, and his brother Leopold from 1872 to 1875. They were not allowed by Queen Victoria to reside in college, so had to live with a private tutor and half a dozen suitable companions elsewhere. Edward lived in Frewin Hall in New Inn Hall Street whilst Leopold lived in St. Giles. They did, however, occasionally dine in Hall.

Leopold must have spent more than a little time in college because he managed to fall in love with the Dean's daughter, Alice Liddel. She was the inspiration for the Alice in Wonderland character, created by the Reverend Charles Dodgson (Lewis Carrol) which had been published in 1865.

Dodgson was a mathematics lecturer at Christ Church as well as being a perpetual curate. He spent his whole working life at Christ Church where he died in 1898, aged sixty-six. As a young man he was shy and retiring but had an empathy with young people, particularly the Dean's daughters of whom Alice was the eldest. He would take them for boat trips on the river where he regaled them with magical tales, in which they all featured. Alice Liddel persuaded Lewis Carrol to write the stories down for her and as a result the stories were published.

Prince Leopold's passion for Alice could not be satisfied as their liaison was forbidden by Queen Victoria on the grounds that as a mere commoner she was unsuitable as a marriage prospect for a Prince of the realm. Leopold was married off to a German Princess but sadly died at the age of thirty. He was an haemophiliac. Alice married another Christ Church student, Reginald Hargreaves. Clearly she must have enjoyed life as the Dean's daughter with its manifold opportunities to meet young men, both suitable and un- suitable.

Leopold, however, is not forgotten at Christ Church because in the Cathedral is a memorial, dedicated *"in affectionate remembrance to Prince Leopold"*.

Interestingly, Alice named her son Leopold and Leopold, named his daughter Alice.

CHRIST CHURCH COLLEGE

Tom Tower by John Doyle

The aphrodisiac of power

John Doyle's view of Tom Tower from Pembroke Square across St. Aldates, dramatically illustrates Christopher Wren's crowning glory to the Christ Church edifice. Also visible through the entrance arch is the statue of Mercury, in the centre of the Great Quadrangle (Tom Quad).

Wren's masterpiece completed, in 1682, Cardinal Thomas Wolsey's western range of building for his original foundation, Cardinal College, which he began in 1525. He was Chancellor to Henry VIII and, next to his monarch, the most powerful man in the land.

Wolsey asset-stripped twenty-two monasteries to provide funds for his new college, which was to be the grandest in all Oxford. Perhaps because it was Oxford's thirteenth foundation it was inevitable that he should fall from grace, having incurred Henry VIII's displeasure for his extravagant use of power. Henry sacked Wolsey in 1529 and took over and finished the new college, renaming it Christ Church in 1546.

Henry VIII suppressed the nearby Osney Abbey and transferred its bell, originally christened Mary, to Christ Church in 1545. It was re-christened Tom in 1612 after Cardinal Thomas Wolsey.

Re-cast in 1680, it weighs more than seven tons and measures more than seven feet in diameter. Because of its enormous size, it became known as Great Tom. It was installed in Wren's newly completed ogee-capped tower in 1682.

CORPUS CHRISTI COLLEGE

The Front Quad by William Matthison

Horology introduced to England

Richard Fox, Bishop of Winchester and Keeper of the Privy Seal for Kings Henry VII and VIII, founded Corpus Christi College in 1517. His original intention was to found a seminary for monks but was persuaded by Hugh Oldham, Bishop of Exeter, to make his new college secular and supported his advice with a handsome donation.

Corpus Christi was the last pre-Reformation college to be founded and the first to make regular provision for the study of classical literature. A tradition which is maintained to this day. One of its most famous students was John Keble, after whom Keble College was named, who gained a double first in Classics and Mathematics, in 1810, at the age of eighteen.

The Pelican, the college emblem taken from Bishop Foxe's coat of arms, can be seen surmounting the column containing the famous sundial. This was erected in 1581 by Charles Turnbull, a Fellow of the College. It celebrates Nicholas Kratzer, a Bavarian who was elected a Fellow of the College in 1517. He introduced horology - the science of measuring - to England.

EXAMINATION SCHOOLS

High Street Front by Hubert Pragnell

Jackson's Masterpiece

Until 1882 examinations were being held in some of the rooms of the ground floor of the School's Quadrangle which was part of Thomas Bodley's Bodleian Library complex. Situated to the north of Radcliffe Square and built between 1613 and 1624 on the site of the mediaeval schools, the term "examination schools" distinguished those buildings used for the purpose.

By the middle of the 19th century there was a demand for increased accomodation for written examinations. At the same time the Bodleian Library was in need of more space. Therefore, it was decided that new examination schools should be built and that the old schools' quadrangle should be handed over to the library.

The replacement Examination Schools in the High Street were built to a design by Sir Thomas Jackson and completed in 1882. This was Jackson's first major work and undoubtedly his finest, even though he was to become, between 1876 and 1914, Oxford's most prolific architect of any period. At Hertford College most of the present buildings are his, including the "Bridge of Sighs" and "Jackson's Spiral Staircase".

The Examination Schools are one of the largest and most adaptable buildings owned by the University and they are home to the University portrait gallery. Its magnificent Great Hall is the setting for many great occasions and it is much used for not only examinations but also lectures. This adaptability was demonstrated in the First World War, when Jackson's Schools became the Third Southern General Hospital. They were also used for a similar purpose during the Second World War.

It is hardly possible to be an undergraduate at Oxford without ever entering the Schools which is the official place for the display of examination results.

Hubert Pragnell
2004

EXETER COLLEGE

Front Quad by Ken Howard

William Morris and The Pre-Raphaelites

Three older colleges, Balliol, Merton and University College, have had a long running dispute as to which is first, second and third in seniority. There is no dispute, however, as to the fact that Exeter is Oxford's fourth oldest college. It was founded in 1314 by Walter de Stapledon, Bishop of Exeter, who rose from humble beginnings to become Edward II's Treasurer. This patronage, however, was to prove fatal, in 1326, when he was beheaded by Edward's enemies. A year later Edward suffered a truly horrific anal execution at Berkeley Castle.

Exeter's omnipresent chapel was completed in 1859 and was the work of the ubiquitous George Gilbert Scott. Its design was based on that of Sainte-Chapelle in Paris. In the chapel hangs a wonderful tapestry designed by Edward Burne-Jones and executed by William Morris, who were contemporaries at Exeter in 1855. At this time they met Dante Gabriel Rossetti and Arthur Hughes, who were leading members of the pre-Raphaelite movement and, after helping them to paint murals on the walls of the University's Woodward debating room, joined them in their quest to return to pre-Raphaelite values. As a result of this decision William Morris gave up his plan to take holy orders and decided on Rossetti's advice to paint, which complimented his burgeoning talent as a poet. He only produced one significant painting, however, "Queen Guinevere" but, in the process discovered his true metier and social gospel, the revival of handicrafts (particularly stained glass) and finally the revolutionizing of the art of house decoration and furnishing in England. To this end he founded, with the help of his pre-Raphaelite associates, the firm of Morris Marshall Faulkner and Company. Later he set up the Kelmscott Press which became legendary for its excellent typography and design in relation to book printing. William Morris died in 1896 aged 62.

EXETER COLLEGE

Front Quad and Hall - William Matthison

Exeter's first 'Saint'

Exeter's greatest benefactor, after its original founder Walter de Stapleton, was William Petre, who rose from humble beginnings in Devonshire, via an Oxford education and government service, to great power and wealth. He survived the religious changes of four reigns to end up as Queen Elizabeth's trusted counsellor.

In 1566, after his retirement from politics, he set about reforming and effectively re-founding his old college. He widened the geographical appeal of the college, from the old Devonian catchment area to include Somerset, Dorset, Oxfordshire and Essex. To fund this he settled the livings of four Oxfordshire rectories. He also revised the college statutes in order to provide a permanent governing hierarchy and formal arrangements for tuition of undergraduates. Petre's munificence saved a failing institution and turned it into a modern college.

During this time of religious upheaval Exeter continued to be strongly Catholic in its sympathies, partly because Petre seemed to have moved in a similarly conservative direction. This was to lead, in 1581, to the execution of Ralph Sherwin, a prominent Fellow who, after a period in Rome, returned to England with Edmund Campion to evangelise the Catholic cause. He was also executed and both were canonized by Paul VI in 1970. As a result, by the early 17th century the college had turned about and became notable for its puritan character.

Then followed Exeter's most prosperous period, when it attracted much outside investment, most notably from Sir John Acland who, in 1618, provided a fine new Hall, noted for its excellent collar-beam roof of Spanish chestnut and good Jacobean oak screen.

William Matthison's painting of Exeter's Front Quadrangle, looking south away from the Chapel, shows the Entrance Tower on the right and the Hall to the left with its fine perpendicular windows and entrance steps.

W. Matthison

GREEN COLLEGE

The Radcliffe Observatory by Jane Carpanini

A tale of three benefactors

During the 1970s plans for a graduate college to be known as Radcliffe College were promulgated, principally by the Regius Professor of Medicine Richard Doll and the Nuffield Professor of Medicine, Paul Beeson. The Radcliffe Observatory and its associated buildings and grounds were allocated for the use of the new college. It was further decided that membership of the new college should be largely confined to Clinical Medicine, although over the years the college has broadened its scope to include facilities which are related to Clinical Medicine, such as Anthropology, Criminology, Education, Environmental Studies and Social Studies.

For the new college to become a reality the Observatory had to be refurbished and new buildings erected. Sir Richard Doll raised £250,000 from various sources including the Radcliffe Trust. This was not nearly enough, however, and a *white knight* in the form of Dr. Cecil Green and his wife Ida arrived on the scene in 1977 and provided a further £2.375 million. Dr. Green was born near Manchester in 1900 and emigrated to the USA when he was two and, during the Second World War, founded Texas Instruments. There is no doubt that without Dr. Green's funding the college would not have been established. So not surprisingly its name became Green College and its first Warden, Sir Richard Doll was appointed in 1979.

There were two much earlier benefactors who indirectly contributed to Green College's conception, the John Radcliffe Trust and Sir William Morris (later Lord Nuffield).

The Radcliffe Trust had originally provided funds for the building of the Radcliffe Infirmary in 1770 and with monies left over funds were provided to build the Radcliffe Observatory next door to the Infirmary. The building was completed in 1794, to a design by James Wyatt, based on The Tower of the Winds in Athens. It has been described as the finest 18th century building in Oxford and by Pevsner as "architecturally the finest observatory in Europe". In its early days the Observatory made notable contributions to astronomy but in 1930 the astronomical institution was moved to Pretoria in South Africa, in search of clearer skies. As a result Sir William Morris bought the Observatory in 1930, on condition that it became a medical research institute within five years. He provided £2 million (£75 million today) and created six Nuffield Professorships in various medical disciplines.

There has always been a close association between the Medical School of the Radcliffe Infirmary and its successor, the John Radcliffe Hospital at Headington and Green College. The Osler House Club originally housed in the old Observer's House has now moved to Headington but, there is still a reciprocity between Green College and the John Radcliffe students. They have joint sports teams and joint social activities.

HERTFORD COLLEGE

Bridge of Sighs by Dennis Flanders

The gay world of Evelyn Waugh

Oxford, between the two World Wars, was a place of rebellion and experimentation. The old order was being challenged by the bright young things of the 1920s. Literature, politics and sex were all areas where free expression was practiced without any due deference to elders.

Ensconced in Hertford, Evelyn was at the forefront of this rebellion. His father, Arthur, was a graduate of New College but his son, Evelyn, won a scholarship to the less fashionable Hertford College. He proceeded, however, to *put it on the map,* so the to speak. His novels, "Decline and Fall" and "Brideshead Revisited" were the quintessential Oxford novels of the period.

Many of the characters in the novel such as Anthony Blanche, the outrageously gay poet, and Lord Sebastian Flyte were based on contemporary acquaintances who were fellow members of the Hypocrities Club, which attracted a lively group of homosexuals. It was closed down in 1923, shortly after Waugh left Oxford. The consequence of opening men's colleges to women in the 1970s clearly helped the English middle class public schoolboys to progress more rapidly from adolescent homosexuality to adult heterosexuality

Evelyn Waugh came from a literary family, his father, Arthur, was managing director of Hall and Chapman, the well-known publishers, whilst his elder brother, Alec attained early distinction with the "Loom of Youth" and later in life "Island in the Sun". There can be no doubt, however, that Evelyn Waugh was one of the finest prose stylists of his generation.

It is pleasing to note that England's two eponymous Bridge of Sighs (the other at St. John's College, Cambridge) are far more beautiful and eyecatching than the original in Venice.

Dennis Flanders.
Hertford College, Oxford

HERTFORD COLLEGE

Catte Street Front by Dennis Roxby Bott

Feline sentiment wins the day

Originally founded as Hart Hall in 1283, it became Hertford College in 1740 but closed in 1818 due to lack of endowments and the site was occupied by Magdalen Hall (1822-1874). In 1874 a noted banker, T.C. Baring, provided a generous endowment which effected the re-founding of Hertford College.

The front of Hertford College can be seen on the left of Dennis Roxby Bott's painting with the Bridge of Sighs just visible to the far left. The thoroughfare onto which Hertford fronts is now known as Catte Street and it runs from Board Street southward to the High.

In Roxby Bott's painting, in the distance, can be seen All Souls on the left, beyond Hertford. On the right, in the foreground, is the Bodleian Library and beyond part of the Radcliffe Camera and Radcliffe Square.

Early spellings included Katterstreete (c1210), Catte Street (1402), Cat Street (18th century). It was once referred to as the *street of mouse catchers* but with the arrival of St. Catherine's Hall to the area, in the 15th century, it was dignified by being called St. Catherine's Street. It being presumed that Cat was the diminutive of Catherine. The poet, Robert Bridges in the 1920s, led a campaign to have the historic "cat" restored. In 1930, Oxford City Council agreed that the name of the street should revert to Cat Street, but with the older spelling of Catte.

JESUS COLLEGE

First Quadrangle by Ken Howard

Elizabeth I—a hidden portrait

Jesus College has been associated with Wales since its foundation by Elizabeth I in 1571, at the petition of Hugh Price, Treasurer of St. David's Cathedral. He provided its first endowments, while the Queen provided the site, buildings and property of White Hall, a redundant academic hall. In fact, it is the only Oxford college to date from the Elizabethan period.

In the Hall there hangs, in pride of place, above High Table, a remarkable full length portrait of Queen Elizabeth I by Nicholas Hilliard (1537-1619) - and thereby hangs a tale.

The painting given to the college by Dr. James Jeffreys, brother of the infamous "hanging judge", mouldered away for centuries in a dark corner of the Fellows' Library, completely unnoticed and un-remarked. It had mainly, in the 17th century, been over-painted and was thought to be just a copy of some unknown contemporary painting and of little value. It was, in effect, a palimpsest.

Then in 1994, the art expert, Alec Cobb, was commissioned to clean the college portraits, including the Charles I portrait by Van Dyck. The Fellows' Library Elizabeth, was not on his list but Mr. Cobb noticed it and was curious. He thought the picture looked interesting and was given permission to bear it away for closer inspection.

After cleaning a section of the painting and submitting it to experts at Christies and Sotheby's it was agreed that it was certainly the work of Nicholas Hilliard, best known for his execution of portrait miniatures. The provenance of the painting was further confirmed by Sir Roy Strong, an acknowledged expert on the paintings of Hilliard.

The over-painting was painstakingly restored, and what had been a forlorn picture in a corner was elevated to the status of a national treasure.

JESUS COLLEGE

The Turl Street Front by Ken Howard

The Turl in Spring

This painting of the Turl Street Front of Jesus College also depicts one of Oxford's landmark views, Turl Street looking towards All Saints Church., which is one of the city's most stylish buildings and forms a stunning climax to Turl Street, with its array of small shops and 15th century Mitre Hotel further up on the right, and the college's of Exeter and Lincoln on the left.

Ken Howard felt that this view was best captured in early Spring before the wonderful Plane tree in the foreground completely obliterated the front of the college. A winter view would have been too stark. Ken's wonderful use of light, his trademark so to speak, is beautifully demonstrated in this picture.

The front of the college shown, is the oldest surviving part of Jesus College, dating from the 16th century, although the tower over the entrance was added in 1854.

Distinguished members of Jesus include Beau Nash (uncrowned "King of Bath"), T. E. Lawrence (Lawrence of Arabia) and former Prime Minister, Harold Wilson. In the ante chapel is a sightless bust of T. E. Lawrence and the college also possesses his campaign notebooks.

KEBLE COLLEGE

The Chapel by Dennis Roxby Bott

Butterfield's masterpiece

Keble College was founded in 1868 by public subscription as a memorial to one person and his work – The Reverend John Keble, M.A., 1792-1866. He was a saintly character who was undoubtedly the catalyst for the foundation of the Anglican High Church, Oxford Movement. He entered Corpus Christi College Oxford, at the age of fourteen and four years later took a Double First in Classics and Mathematics, a brilliant feat rarely achieved. He was immediately elected a Fellow at Oriel and spent time as a parish priest in Hampshire. He returned to Oxford in 1831 to take up the post of Professor of Poetry.

Contrary to popular belief Keble College was not intended as a seminary for the Anglo Catholic priesthood. Its purpose was to provide, under Church of England auspices, a university education for men of ability but limited means. It was a somewhat austere secular college with students living in only one room and taking all their meals in Hall.

William Butterfield (1814-1900) was hired as architect and his redbrick gothic masterpiece has caused controversy ever since. The new college was unlike any other in Oxford with its idiosyncratic use of bricks of different colours. You either love it or you loathe it, according to your taste. John Betjeman loved it. Butterfield even sank the centre of the Liddon Quadrangle to give his buildings an increased sense of height. It was considered to be highly original although, Verona and its eleventh and twelfth century brick and tufa churches may have provided inspiration.

The interior of the Chapel is decorated with mosaics illustrating events from the Old and New Testaments and in the side Chapel hangs William Holman Hunt's painting "The Light of the World".

KEBLE COLLEGE

Liddon Quad by Dennis Roxby Bott

H. M. Postmaster General bans college stamps

Colleges had always used a messenger service for delivering letters locally. The book-keeping involved, however, was horrendous as the charges for delivery had to be entered on the senders battels (account for board and lodging and other expenses).

In order to save the cost of entering such trivial amounts Keble, in 1871, decided to issue its own stamps on letters or messages delivered within the centre of Oxford. The scheme was so successful that seven other colleges followed suit. All Souls, Balliol, Exeter, Hertford, Lincoln, Merton and St. Johns.

The first stamps bore the college coat of arms and the words "Keble * College * Oxon" in an oval. Each stamp also bore the name of the printer, Spier & Son, High Street, Oxford, at the foot of the stamp.

On the 28th January, 1886, the Postmaster General, however, objected that the system was an infringement of the Post Offices monopoly. The use of college stamps was thus curtailed. They had been in use for nearly fifteen years but examples of them are rare and are much sought after by philatelists. Keble continued to use franked envelopes until the 1890s.

It would be interesting to know whether Keble's venture into postal services had been profitable.

Dennis Roxby Bott's view of Liddon Quad is unusual, inasmuch, as it is forever associated with the chapel. Dennis has, however, highlighted the other aspects, the Gate-Tower on the left and the Hall in the centre.

LADY MARGARET HALL

LMH -Garden by Dennis Roxby Bott

Invasion of the women

Not only were Oxford's colleges inhabited entirely by male undergraduates, until dons were permitted to marry in 1877, but few women graced the Fellows' Gardens or Masters' Lodgings. However, with the foundation in 1878 of the first women's residential hall, Lady Margaret Hall (LMH) women began to "invade" what had been an entirely male preserve.

The foundress was Elizabeth Wordsworth, daughter of the Bishop of Lincoln and a great niece of the poet, William Wordsworth. She named the college after Lady Margaret Beaufort, mother of Henry VII, who had founded two Cambridge colleges, in the early part of the 16th century, Christ's and St. John's. Both Elizabeth Wordsworth's father and brother were Bishops and the first Chairman of LMH was Edward Talbot, Warden of Keble, that bastion of the Anglican high church. It was not surprising, therefore, that only members of the Church of England were admitted to the college. The last religious restrictions were not removed until 1871 and in 1979 men were admitted to LMH, thus making it fully emancipated, both religiously and sexually.,

In 1893 an eight acre tract of land running down to the river Cherwell was purchased from St. John's College. The first buildings on it were designed by Sir Reginald Blomfield and erected between 1896 and 1915 in pleasing red brick. They were named Wordsworth, Talbot and Lodge. The extensive gardens, stretching down to the Cherwell are a timeless and attractive feature.

Roxby Bott

LINACRE COLLEGE

College Entrance by Hubert Pragnell

Founder of the Royal College of Physicians

Linacre College was established by the University in 1962 to address concerns about graduates of other universities finding a congenial environment in which to read for advanced degrees.

The move of St. Catherine's to its new site left vacant the buildings below Christ Church gardens in St. Aldates Street. All students lived in lodgings since the buildings had no residential accommodation. This deficiency was corrected when the college moved to a much larger but older building on the corner of South Parks Road and St. Cross Road, known as Cherwell Edge, which had been designed by Basil Champneys.

The necessary conversion and extension of Cherwell Edge was facilitated by the generosity of old members and grants from various Trusts and Foundations. A new main entrance and large dining hall were accordingly added to the building and in 1985 a second residential block, Bamborough Building was completed, named after the college's first Principal, J. B. Bamborough. This building like the other additions was designed by the University Surveyor, Jack Lankester, in a congruent "Queen Anne" style, matching Basil Champneys original.

Hubert Pragnell's painting clearly illustrates the original part of the Cherwell Edge building to the right and the homogeneous additions to the left.

The college takes its name from Thomas Linacre, a distinguished classical scholar, who was elected a Fellow of All Souls in 1484, at the age of 24. He travelled widely in Italy and obtained a medical degree at the University of Padua. On his return to England he obtained Letters Patent from Henry VII to regulate the practice of medicine, which led to the foundation of The Royal College of Physicians. His pupils included Sir Thomas Moore and Erasmus who, along with Cardinal Wolsey, became his patients when he established himself as a Physician in London. He was also King's Physician to Henry VII and Henry VIII.

A distinctive feature of Linacre College is its truly international flavour, with a large proportion of its post graduate students coming from overseas.

LINCOLN COLLEGE

College Front by William Matthison

The Cradle of Methodism

Lincoln is Oxford's eighth oldest college, having been founded in 1427 by Richard Fleming, Bishop of Lincoln, in which diocese Oxford was then included. Oxford became a separate diocese in 1542.

Richard Fleming had initially been a follower of John Wycliffe and his Lollard movement, whose views were held to be heretical because they questioned the worldliness and corruption of the Church. Moreover, they encouraged the use of the vernacular bible, which Wycliffe had translated into English in the lat 14th century. At this time many of Oxford's leading Lollards were excommunicated and were forced to recant and Fleming, in an act of atonement, founded Lincoln College, for the special purpose of suppressing Lollardism.

It is by a curious irony of fate that the college, in the 18th century, became the birthplace Methodism during the residence of John Wesley. From 1726 until 1735 he occupied rooms in Chapel Quad, during which time the Holy Club was set up. He departed for Georgia in the USA as a Missionary Chaplain in 1735. He remained a Fellow until 1751 when he married (Fellows in Oxford were not permitted to marry until 1877).

The room where Wycliffe gave his tutorials is on the first floor of Staircase Two, in the south-east corner of the Front Quad, from where the painting opposite was made. Although it remains a tutor's room it is vacated every afternoon so that visitors may see it. In 1926 to commemorate the 200th anniversary of Wesley's election to a fellowship, Methodists in America paid for 15th century linenfold panelling to be installed, together with 18th century furniture.

W. Matthison

LINCOLN COLLEGE

The All Saints Library by Jane Carpanini

Another Radcliffe benefaction

On The High at the end of Turl Street is one of Oxford's landmarks, All Saints Church, which was founded in the 12th century. The present building dates from 1720 and was the work of the great amateur architect, Henry Aldrich, Dean of Christ Church and Nicholas Hawksmoor, a protégé of Christopher Wren. In fact, All Saints has been described as an academic version of a Wren church of the simpler type.

In 1896 All Saints succeeded St. Martin's Carfax as the City Church, under the patronage of Lincoln College, until it was declared redundant in 1971. St. Michael's at the Northgate is now the City Church.

Having been declared redundant as a church, it was decided to convert All Saints into a library for Lincoln College, under the supervision of Robert Potter. Re-roofing was carried out and eroded stone replaced, carved by the Stonemason of Chichester Cathedral using stone from Besace near Cambrai. Inside, the nave floor was raised four feet six inches to provide a lower reading room and the former Senior Library was moved, complete, into the lower east end of the building.

The conversion, completed in 1975, cost £420,000 and a generous contribution was received from the John Radcliffe estate. He was one of Lincoln's most distinguished Fellows (1670-75), whose benefactions named after him - the Radcliffe Camera, Radcliffe Infirmary and the Radcliffe Observatory - adorn the city. He was a wealthy doctor and physician to Queen Anne. He even had a quadrangle built and named after him at University College.

It seems odd that Radcliffe's benefactions did not extend to his own college until 1975. This probably had something to do with the fact that Lincoln refused to dispense him from the obligation of taking Holy Orders so forcing his resignation in 1675. Three hundred years later his Trustees were more forgiving.

Jane Carpanini's meticulous painting illustrates the true beauty and grace of this most impressive conversion; showing to good effect the classical columns, tall clear-glazed windows and fine woodwork. Fortunately this can be appreciated by the widest possible audience because, uniquely among working college libraries, it is open to the public two afternoons a week.

MAGDALEN COLLEGE

Bell Tower by Ken Messer

Oscar Wilde and other men of controversy

Magdalen College was founded in 1458 and its Bell Tower which dominates the painting opposite is one of the outstanding landmarks of Oxford.

Its founder, William Wayneflete, was not only Bishop of Winchester but also Provost of Eton College. He was a skilled politician with a particular interest in education because, he also became Headmaster of Winchester College. He was one of the trio of negotiators along with Stafford, Archbishop of Canterbury and Cardinal Kempe who negotiated with the so called Jack Cade to end the 1450 rebellion bearing his name.

Wayneflete was a devoted Lancastrian and in the negotiations with the rebel leader John Mortimer, a cousin of the Duke of York, somehow, changed his name to Jack Cade. Thus revoking his pardon granted to all the rebels. An act of treachery that was to forever have him in trouble with the later victorious Yorkists.

Another controversial figure associated with Magdalen was Oscar Wilde, who gained a double first and loved his time at Oxford *"the most beautiful thing in England",* apart from his professors. He was always at loggerheads with the dons who at every opportunity sought to put down this precocious genius. He has, however, given more pleasure to the world than all the dons put together. His parting remark to a fellow undergraduate was "Somehow or other I'll be famous and if not notorious". Being Wilde he succeeded in being both.

C. S. Lewis was a Fellow at Magdalen for over 30 years and went on to write popular religious and moral books including "The Screwtape Letters". He is best remembered, however, for his children's books such as "The Lion and the Witch and the Wardrobe". Lewis was a highly successful lecturer at Oxford but he was passed over for the Merton Chair of English Literature in 1946; and on being appointed in 1954 to a newly established chair in English Mediaeval and Renaissance Literature at Cambridge he left Magdalen Oxford for Magdalene Cambridge.

Another great man of letters to attend Magdalen was Poet Laureate, John Betjeman, who was sent down in 1926 without taking a degree for failing to pass a qualifying examination and to please his tutors - on of whom was C. S. Lewis!

MANSFIELD COLLEGE

The Quad by Ken Messer

Non-conformists liberated

The abolition of religious tests in 1871 brought students from the Free churches into Oxford colleges, where they could study for arts degrees. As a result in 1886 Spring Hill Theological College in Birmingham decided to move to Oxford. It was renamed Mansfield College after the family who had originally founded Spring Hill in 1838. There were, at this time, a considerable number of Non-conformists in the university and many of these felt that the Free churches must have a more organized vigorous and yet academic approach. It was in this climate that Mansfield evolved.

The ubiquitous Basil Champneys was retained as architect and together with George Faulkner Armitage designed and constructed the buildings and their furnishings. The buildings were designed in the best collegiate Gothic style. It was meant to blend in with its Oxford setting; to become a seamless addition when completed in 1889.

The chapel on the right in Ken Messer's painting has beautiful oak and stone carving and its stained glass was designed by Edward Burn-Jones and executed by William Morris. The great organ was built by W. G. Vowks of Bristol and was a firm favourite of Dr. Albert Schweitzer when he was at the college as Dale Lecturer in 1934. The Hall and Senior Common Room are located to the right of the tower and these rooms have recently been refurbished in a way which will retain their late Victorian style.

Although the college has retained close ties with Reformed and Lutheran churches and many traditions including Anglican, Roman Catholic and Orthodox, 80% of its students now study secular subjects.

MERTON COLLEGE

View from Christ Church Meadow by John Doyle

Dead Man's Walk – the Jewish connection

The painting opposite is a view from across the rear of Merton College with the spire of Christ Church Cathedral clearly visible to the left. To the right on the other side of Dead Man's Walk are the remains of the old 12th century City Wall; the only significant portion left, after those in New College. Dead Man's Walk is so called because it was the route taken by Jewish funeral processions from St. Aldates, the site of the Synagogue, to their burial ground in what is now the Botanic Garden. It was just outside the city walls and, therefore, considered, until 1290, a respectable place for Jews to be buried. After that date in the face of frequent charges of extortion and "coin clipping", Edward I barred Jews from England altogether. They did not return until the 17th century at the behest of Oliver Cromwell.

Merton still has a dispute with Balliol and University College as to seniority and it depends on which basis, judgement is made. If the criterion, however, is which college was first to have a resident student population, then Merton is the oldest. It was founded in 1264 by Walter de Merton, later Bishop of Rochester, and was the model upon which the first Cambridge college, Peterhouse, was founded by the Bishop of Ely in 1282. University College and Balliol claim to have been founded in 1249 and 1263 respectively.

MERTON COLLEGE

Merton Street by John Doyle

Zuleika – The ultimate femme fatale

A distinguished Merton alumnus was Sir Beerbohm 1872-1956, a humorist, essayist and cartoonist of international renown. He was born in London and entered Merton College in 1890 where he occupied rooms in Mob Quad until 1894. His precocious talent and anarchic wit was wonderfully in tune with the time and he began, in 1895, publishing caricatures in the Strand Magazine and essays in the Yellow Book. The latter were published collectively under the somewhat facetious title "The Works of Max Beerbohm" in 1896.

However his true masterpiece was "Zuleika Dobson" a satirical novel published in 1911 and alternatively titled "An Oxford Love Story". "Zuleika the eponymous heroine decides to visit her grand-father, the Warden of Judas during Eights Week. She is so ravishing that on her arrival in Oxford as the landau rolled by sweat started to pour from the brows of the Emperors (the landmark fourteen stone heads standing in front of the Sheldonian). All the undergraduates in Oxford fall madly in love with her including the splendid and haughty Duke of Dorset. The Duke fulfils his somewhat rash promise to lay down his life for her by drowning himself and is followed by the entire undergraduate population who plunge into the Isis like lemmings with great cries of "Zuleika". That evening Zuleika asks her maid to consult Bradshaw to see if it is possible to go direct from here to Cambridge!

Max Beerbohm was knighted in 1939, although from 1910 at the time of his marriage he lived mainly in Italy. He returned home during the two world wars and established a reputation as a broadcaster.

Interestingly in 1952 Beerbohm gave permission for Sir Osbert Lancaster to paint twelve scenes from his Zuleika novel for the Randolph Hotel. He even suggested which scenes might be chosen and hoped that the poor Emperors heads would not be ignored. They were not. The pictures still hang in the hotel in the Lancaster Suite.

John Doyle had long wanted to paint the view looking west along Merton Street ever since he had seen a similar view by J. M. W. Turner, painted in 1838 and which hangs in the Tate Gallery. This mediaeval street scene is timeless showing, not only the front of Merton but also the tower of Corpus Christi at the end of Merton Street.

John Doyle.

NEW COLLEGE

The Great Quad by Dennis Roxby Bott

The prototype quadrangle

When founded in 1379, William of Wykeham's College, the seventh oldest in Oxford, was known as The St. Mary College of Winchester in Oxford. There was already, however, another college in Oxford dedicated to St. Mary - Oriel College. As a result, William of Wykeham's foundation became known as New College.

There are two main points of entry into New College. The original entrance into the Great Quad was down New College Lane. This is now the visitors' entrance where an admission fee is charged. The working entrance with Porter's Lodge is in Holywell Street.

The Great Quad contained all the principal buildings, essential to the communal life envisaged by the founder, including chapel, hall and library. It was the prototype quadrangle upon which many subsequent foundations were based, including those in Cambridge where, of course, they are called Courts.

Dennis was keen to produce a watercolour of the Great Quad, through the original New College Lane gate-tower entrance. This would enable him to frame his painting with the archway entrance, showcasing on the left the eastern end of the chapel, the Muniment Tower with its entrance to the Hall and in the centre of the painting, the Founder's Library with an archway leading to the college gardens.

NEW COLLEGE

Gaude Night by Cliff Bayly

A convivial return

The word quaudy or gaude comes from the Latin word gaudere meaning to rejoice. It was used from the Elizabethan period to describe the Freshmen dinner but by the 17th century it had a wider usage, covering any college commemorative feast.

Such gaudies are now widespread throughout the colleges and give alumni or old members an opportunity to return to their college to spend a convivial evening eating and drinking. They are usually arranged in year groups so that contemporaries can meet again. The time interval between such gaudy nights is seven to ten years and they are held in both winter and summer.

New College has adopted the spelling gaude and arranges for a section of the college's choir to stand on the steps leading up to the Hall to sing a summons. The members make their way round the Great Quad to listen, before proceeding up the steps and into the Hall.

In Cliff Bayly's painting the Choir has done its job and old members are clearly enjoying the food and drink and re-engaging with old acquaintances.

NEW COLLEGE

New College Lane by John Doyle

Away from the madding crowds

One of the most delightful short sections of thoroughfare in Oxford is the 500 metres or so, covered by New College Lane and Queen's Lane from Catte Street, by the Sheldonian, to the High Street opposite the Examination Schools. The only vehicles permitted along this byway are bicycles, so one experiences a sense of timelessness as well as peace and tranquillity.

Commencing at Catte Street you pass under the Bridge of Sighs and pass on the left St. Helen's Passage and the Turf Tavern. Just before the first turn to the right and in front of the partly obscured Bell Tower of New College there is, on the left, No. 6 New College Lane (just visible in the painting opposite, to the left of the red brick building), the home of Edmund Halley from 1703 to 1742. The best known comet in the universe is named after him. He had his observatory next door at No. 7 and he was, at the time, Savilian Professor of Geometry.

After this first bend in New College Lane there is another to the left, which is in the nature of a cul-de-sac leading to the old entrance to New College. (Since 1982 the official entrance has been from Holywell Street, which contains the main Porters Lodge). In Dennis Roxby Bott's painting on page 71 the old entrance and the Great Quad beyond can be viewed to great effect.

A third bend under a mini Bridge of Sighs arch, in front of New College's old Porters Lodge, takes us into Queen's Lane, which after a fourth bend to the left, then runs between the rear of New College on the left and Queen's on the right. The final twist to the right takes us past the redundant church of St. Peter's in the East and the somewhat obscure entrance to St. Edmund Hall, on the right, before discourging us into the busy High Street.

ORIEL COLLEGE

Front Quadrangle by Ken Howard

A lesson in composition

In Ken Howard's painting the Hall can be viewed immediately in front, through the arch of the entrance gateway from Oriel Square. It is approached up a small flight of steps under an open portico. Above the portico can be seen the words *Regnante Carolo* referring to Charles I, during whose reign the Hall was built. During the Civil War Charles I used Oxford as his campaign headquarters until his surrender in 1646. He used Oriel for meetings of the Privy Council.

In painting, effective compositions can come about through unexpected changes in the weather. Ken Howard was driven by persistent rainfall to shelter in the entrance gateway and he was struck by the pleasing effect of reflections in the puddles across the Front Quad. Ken commented that the combination of light, water and reflections is the reason painters never tire of Venice. He also observed that duller days, are, in some ways, more preferable because it is more consistent in terms of shadows and that bright sunlight does not bring out all the subtle colours in the stonework; it drowns them in light.

ORIEL COLLEGE

Wyatt Library by Ken Howard

Birthplace of the Oxford Movement

Although the present early 17th century front quadrangle of Oriel was one of the largest building projects to be realized in pre-Restoration Oxford, its architect is unknown. The second quadrangle, however, is dominated by a magnificent 18th century neo-classical library and common room beneath, whose architect is definitely identifiable; James Wyatt, more famous for the doomed Fonthill Abbey in Wiltshire, 1795-1812 and, of course, the Radcliffe Observatory.

Oriel was founded under licence from King Edward II in 1326, so can claim to be the first college to boast a royal founder. He also gifted a large house, La Oriole, from which the college takes its name. This stood on the site of the present Front Quadrangle and was so called because of its "oratoriolum" or projecting window, hence the term oriel window.

The Oxford Movement was founded at Oriel in 1833 by four of its Fellows, John Keble, J. H. Newman, R. H. Froude and E. B. Pusey. Its purpose was to return the Anglican Church to the more conservative values or *catholic* doctrines of the early Fathers. They were also known as Tractarians, as a result of the ninety or so "tracts" published under Newman's authorship. Public feeling was against the Movement and it finally broke up in 1845.

Another famous alumnus was Cecil Rhodes who made a huge fortune in southern Africa in the 1880's. Rhodesia was named after him.

PEMBROKE COLLEGE

Old Quad by Dennis Roxby Bott

Enlightened self-interest

The quaint Old Quadrangle, the first you enter, dates from 1627-1670 and is the oldest part of the college, although modernized by the Victorians.

Pembroke was founded in 1624 and named after the Chancellor of the University at the time, William Herbert, Third Earl of Pembroke. It was however, two Abingdon men, Thomas Teesdale and Richard Whightwick who provided the "where with all" to found a college, principally, to receive students from Abingdon School.

Balliol had originally been offered these endowments in return for securing places for Abingdon men but, had rather haughtily, refused the bribe, although goodness knows why, such arrangements had been quite common in mediaeval times.

James I, always interested in academic matters, immediately granted Letters Patent to found a new college and enhance his reputation as a supporter of the arts and learning.

Pembroke's most famous alumnus was probably Samuel Johnson who was at the college for just a year in 1728. He rebelled against its oppressive regime and left without taking a degree. Even so, he held his *alma mater* in great affection returning many times and, in 1775, received an Honorary Doctorate from the University.

Pembroke College also educated Sir Philip Sidney and was the inspiration for Thackery's "Pendennis", published in 1849 and renamed St. Boniface.

Roxby Bott

QUEEN'S COLLEGE

Queen's over the Roofs by Dennis Flanders

American anglophile

This is a most unusual view of Queen's College from the top of the Goodhart Building, which is part of University College (Univ).

The magnificence of William Townesend's entrance screen and cupola of 1734, based on designs by Nicholas Hawksmoor, can just be seen over the roofs of Univ on the other side of the High Street. It was based on the Luxembourg Palace in Paris. What can be seen quite clearly behind the entrance screen, is the Palladian Front Quadrangle, thought by Pevsner to be the finest example of classical architecture in Oxford.

Dennis' over-riding memory of this work, undertaken in 1962, was the hospitality of the Master of University College, Professor Arthur Goodhart, from whose penthouse suite Dennis made this watercolour.

Arthur Goodhart was born in New York and attended Yale University before coming to Britain to attend Trinity College, Cambridge. He was a great anglophile who, although spending most of his working life in Oxford, never became anglicised. He was a distinguished lawyer who occupied the Chair of Jurisprudence at Oxford from 1931-1951. He was University College's greatest benefactor and was its Master from 1951-1963. He was made an honorary K.B.E., in 1948, for his diplomatic achievements in helping gain American support for Britain during the early part of the Second World War and died in 1978, aged 87.

His eldest son is Sir Philip Goodhart, the former Member of Parliament for Beckenham, who has one of the largest private collections of Dennis Flanders' work of which this is one.

ST. EDMUND HALL

Front Quadrangle by William Matthison

Last remaining mediaeval Hall

Turning off The High into Queen's Lane and taking the second door on the right, one enters the higgledy piggledy quadrangle of St. Edmund Hall, which is an absolute delight.

The college takes its name from St. Edmund of Abingdon, who reputedly lived and lectured here in the late 12th century. He later became Archbishop of Canterbury (1234-1240) but his embryo did not became a college until 1957 due to lack of endowments. It is, in fact, the last surviving mediaeval hall in Oxford - those halls in which students lived before the establishment of residential colleges, as we know them today.

Willaim Matthison's painting from 1907 depicts a scene that has hardly changed for three hundred years. Facing, is the chapel, constructed in the classical style (in 1682) by Stephen Penton,. Over the ante-chapel, Penton built the hall's first library, which was the first in Oxford to have shelves along the walls. The cottage to the right of the chapel dates from the early 17th century. The buildings to the left, with the three dormers, beyond the sundial, were constructed in the late 16th century.

There is one change to the scene depicted because in 1927, in the centre of the grassed area, the ancient well was opened up and fitted with a new head over it.

St. Edmund Hall is affectionately known as Teddy Hall and long before they became generally available teddy bears were marketed by the college as souvenirs.

ST. HILDA'S COLLEGE

The River Cherwell by Jane Carpanini

Dames' delight and Parson's pleasure

The River Cherwell has its source five miles south of Daventry in Northamptonshire and flows for a total of 35 miles before it joins the Thames (or Isis as it is called for its Oxford span) below Christ Church Meadow. Unlike the Isis commercial exploitation has not been visited upon the Cherwell. It is essentially a river reserved for pleasure being too narrow and shallow for competitive rowing. Pleasure in this instance not confined to punting or rowing but also swimming, albeit in sometimes controversial manner.

Swimming took place initially at a dammed up pool, just below the University Parks, called Parson's Pleasure. This had been since the 17th century reserved for male bathers only and was screened from view when men took to sunbathing and bathing in the nude. This practice has now been abandoned and the area is no longer boarded. Its site can be seen immediately to the left over the bridge by Linacre College.

In 1934 women secured their own area close by for uninhibited bathing called Dames' Delight. This too was screened but was closed in 1970 due to flood damage.

Jane Carpanini's nostalgic painting of the Cherwell at Milham Ford depicts a scene that is timeless in its peace and serenity.

ST. HUGH'S COLLEGE

College Gardens by Cliff Bayly

The Wordsworth and Lincoln connections

Between 1878 and 1893 the five Oxford women's colleges were founded, following the University Reform Act of 1877 which was the result of twenty years of liberalization initiated by William Gladstone and Benjamin Jowett. One of these colleges was St. Hugh's, founded in 1886 by Elizabeth Wordsworth who had also founded Lady Margaret Hall in 1879; the first ladies college. She is the only person in Oxford to have founded two colleges.

Dame Elizabeth Wordsworth, as she later became, was a grand-niece of the poet William Wordsworth and daughter of the Bishop of Lincoln. Interestingly, she named the college after St. Hugh, an eminent 12th century Bishop of Lincoln, renowned for his success in the promotion of learning and a favourite of Henry II.

Until 1916, St. Hugh's resided at various houses in Norham Gardens, off the Banbury Road, in North Oxford. In 1916, on a site between the Banbury and Woodstock Roads, the first custom built college for women was completed. It was designed by H. T. Buckland and W. Haywood in, what Pevsner calls, "symmetrical neo Georgian". All red brick except for two lodges which are of stone. The building is large and has its true façade to the garden. It has two projecting wings and many pretty bow windows on the ground floor.

The gardens are among the most extensive and beautiful in Oxford, covering some 14 acres. The main lawn and wooded areas have been designated a garden of historical interest. They include The Dell, a Victorian fernery which was part of the gardens of The Mount, the grand house demolished to make way for the new college, a nut walk and a wilderness of the same date run along the southern boundary. A magnolia tree planted for the armistice, after the First World War in 1918 is a striking feature on the front lawn.

Clifford Bayly

ST. JOHN'S COLLEGE

St. Giles Front by John Doyle

A tale of four martyrs

The busy front of St. John's College is conveniently set back from the road and enjoys the distinction, once shared by other colleges, of a terrace-walk shaded with plane trees facing its main entrance.

St. John's was originally founded by Archbishop Chichele in 1437 as the St. Bernard College for Cistercian students. It was dissolved in 1539 during the Reformation, along with other monastic institutions and its site given to Henry VIII's own college, Christ Church. After Henry's death a wealthy Roman Catholic Clothier purchased the site and buildings, in 1555, to found St. John's College in gratitude for the restoration of Catholicism under Mary I. There then followed a truly bloody period in Oxford history as religious controversy ensued.

The most notable event is commemorated by the martyrs memorial, just visible behind the elm tree in John Doyle's painting. It was the architect, George Gilbert Scott's first work in Oxford, completed in 1843 to commemorate three prominent Protestants, Bishops Latimer, Ridley and Archbishop Cranmer, being burnt at the stake in Broad Street in 1555 and 1556. The memorial is in St. Giles and not Broad Street because the former is a more prominent position. When Mary was succeeded by her Protestant sister, Elizabeth, the tide turned and one of St. John's first Fellows, Edward Campion, became Oxford's most celebrated Catholic martyr when, in 1581, he was executed at Tyburn. Thereafter, Roman Catholics were not officially allowed to attend the University until 1895.

ST. PETER'S COLLEGE

Emily Morris Building by Jane Carpanini

The Chavasse connection

Lord Nuffield (William Morris), the car maker, was a great benefactor, who redeemed the college's onerous mortgage in the 1930s, not long after its foundation in 1929, and provided the Emily Morris building in memory of his mother.

The Chavasse family are central to the foundation and development of St. Peter's College. Founded by Francis Chavasse, the Bishop of Liverpool, the college takes its name from the Church of St. Peter-le-Bailey, where Francis Chavasse had been Rector (1879-1899). His son, Christopher, who was also Rector of St. Peter's from 1927-1939, became the college's first Master in 1929. His father had died in 1928.

In 1935 the church was closed due to parish amalgamations and became the Chapel of St. Peter's College.

It had been designed by Basil Champneys in 1874 to replace an earlier church and explains why the college has a somewhat over-large college chapel. Nonetheless it is quite magnificent and has recently been adorned by some fine stained glass by the late refugee artist, Ervin Bossanyi. They are the prototypes of his famous windows in Canterbury Cathedral and are a gift to the college from his family.

SEWANEE - THE UNIVERSITY OF THE SOUTH

The Quad by Ken Howard

Exporting Oxford

In the 1998 Hilary issue of the University magazine, "Oxford Today", an article appeared under the heading *Exporting Oxford.* Its purpose was to explore attempts throughout the world to imitate Oxford's (shared with Cambridge) unique collegiate system. The article examined attempts elsewhere, principally America, Australia and New Zealand, to replicate the Oxford model, but more or less concluded that Oxford was inimitable.

One of the universities examined was the University of the South, Sewanee, situated in Tennessee, 90 miles south of Nashville. It was founded in 1857 out of a need by the Episcopal Church to found a University in the southern states. Money was raised and a foundation stone laid on land donated by the Sewanee Mining Company at a place known to the Indians as Sewanee.

Before any meaningful construction work had begun, however, the disastrous Civil War engulfed the country. Funds raised were diverted to help the Confederate's war effort. After the war, the south was devastated but, the Bishop of Tennessee returned to the campus in 1866 to formally re-establish the University. Money was raised from many quarters including Oxford University and its colleges. To this day Sewanee, as the university is popularly known, continues to be owned by 28 Episcopal diocese in 12 southern states.

The integrity of its Gothic architecture is amazing. One of its earliest structures, the Breslin Tower (1886) was modelled on Magdalen Tower, Oxford and all subsequent buildings have remained faithful to the gothic style.

As a result of the Oxford Today article I contacted Sewanee's Alumni Relations Department and suggested that they should, like Oxford's colleges, participate in our watercolour print series. They readily agreed and it was arranged that Ken Howard should visit and produce three watercolour paintings. Ken spent a delightful week in Sewanee's campus, which is situated 2,500 feet above sea level, on a plateau in central Tennessee. Its campus is an oasis of tranquillity set in 10,000 acres of the most delightful woodland, with breathtaking views all around. Sewanee students study the liberal arts and its student population is limited to 1,400 with a teacher pupil ratio of 9:1. It has always had close links with the Church of England and Oxford University, having summer schools each year in both Lincoln College and St. John's College.

The painting featured opposite is of the three sided quadrangle, looking towards the cupola topped Carnegie Hall, which was completed in 1913. To the left with its cloisters is the Walsh Ellett Hall, completed in 1886. Also in the painting the choir can be seen processing across the front of the Carnegie Hall on their way to the magnificent All Saints Chapel which is just out of the picture, to the right.

It is just as well Sewanee has its own stonemason's yard on site because building in the gothic style continues with a new $12,000,000 Dining Hall completed in 2000.

SHELDONIAN THEATRE

Degree Ceremony by Cliff Bayly

A Theatre for all occasions

The Sheldonian Theatre is the principal assembly room of the University. All public ceremonies of the University are performed here, notably the annual Enceania when honorary degrees are conferred, and the twenty or so Degree ceremonies which are held each year.

For centuries such ceremonies were held in the University Church of St. Mary the Virgin. However, because the Encaenia was a social, as well as an academic occasion, strict churchmen thought it inappropriate that a wholly secular, and often noisy ceremony, should take place in a sacred building. To assuage these concerns the Archbishop of Canterbury, Gilbert Sheldon, in 1664, commissioned the Sheldonian Theatre to serve as a place for the enactment of university business and ceremonies. Sheldon provided about £14,500 for the building. The architect chosen being Christopher Wren, who was at that time Savilian Professor of Astronomy. It was Wren's first major architectural work. The theatre was completed in 1669 and named after Gilbert Sheldon, who had earlier been Warden of All Souls and since 1667, Chancellor of the University.

The name and design of the building are derived from the Roman amphitheatres, open to the sky, and the painted ceiling by Robert Streater expresses this characteristic. A theatre open to the sky, however, clearly would not be practical in an English setting, so the permanent shelter of a roof would be needed. To introduce load bearing columns would ruin the resemblance to a theatre, so Wren, with the help of scientific friends, came up with a specially designed truss that would support the 70 foot span of the roof. This technical ingenuity was concealed from below by Streaters painted ceiling.

In Cliff Bayly's painting the magnificence of Wren's amphitheatre design can be seen to full effect with all the pomp and circumstance of a Degree Ceremony. In the painting we see the candidates for the Degree of Master of Arts returning to the theatre having donned their distinctive red gowns after their initial presentation to the Vice Chancellor and Proctors.

Tiered seats accommodate up to 2,000 people and the columns of the gallery are painted to resemble marble. The Theatre is now also used for lectures and Concerts and Haydn's Symphony No. 92 will forever be associated with the Sheldonian. It was composed in 1788 and performed in 1791, when the composer was in Oxford to receive the honorary degree of Doctor of Music. It has been known as the "Oxford Symphony" since that time.

Clifford Bayly

SOMERVILLE COLLEGE

The Garden Quad by Jane Carpanini

Three cerebral women

Until 1994 Somerville, the second oldest ladies' foundation (1879) in Oxford, was one of the two remaining female-only colleges in Oxford. Since the last war, it has produced two lady prime ministers, Indira Gandhi (India 1966) and Margaret Thatcher (Great Britain 1979). In addition, other distinguished scholars include P. D. James, Iris Murdoch, Shirley Williams, Esther Rantzen and the Nobel Prize winner, Dorethy Hodgkin.

One morning in the spring of 1988, I heard the Principal of the College, Daphne Park, being interviewed on Radio 4 about her fund-raising trip to America. I later telephoned her to see if we could channel her fund-raising zeal towards the production of limited edition prints of Somerville. Once she realized that financially there was no *downside potential* (an Americanism appropriate to one returning from the States) for the College, she readily agreed. In fact, Somerville was our first Oxford project.

Daphne Park had spent much of her working life in the service of government in the diplomatic and intelligence field. Her physical appearance, a small, well-rounded Miss Marple with a kindly demeanour, seemed to contradict her former profession. This was partly the reason she was so successful in her chosen career.

In 1996 Dame Fiona Caldicott became Principal. She is President of the Royal College of Psychiatrists.

Another distinguished alumnus was Dorothy L. Sayers who, in 1935 published "Gaudy Night" - the most celebrated portrayal of life in a women's college.

TRINITY COLLEGE

Broad Street Front by William Matthison

An adroit Tudor politician

The entrance to Trinity is between the stone piers and handsome ironwork of the gates. To the right in William Matthison's early twentieth century painting are the quaint old cottages that have been transformed into a porters' lodge. This view has not changed in over 100 years, with the exception of the low railings to the right, now replaced with a wall.

The open and spacious Front Quadrangle, laid to lawn with mature trees around its perimeter, is quite different from any other in terms of visual accessibility. In the background is the first non-gothic chapel to be constructed in Oxford, when in 1694, it replaced the earlier 13th century Durham College chapel.

Trinity was founded by Sir Thomas Pope in 1555 in gratitude for the restoration of Catholicism under Mary Tudor. He was clearly an adroit politician because he served her father, Henry VIII, and brother, Edward VI. As Treasurer of the Court of Augmentation, it was his job to gather together the estates of the monasteries dissolved at the Reformation. In the process he amassed for himself a considerable fortune, part of which he used to purchase the site and buildings of one of the dissolved monastic foundations, Durham College. This became Trinity College.

Sir Thomas Pope was also a guardian of Mary's sister, Princess Elizabeth, at Hatfield House, and she found his company most congenial.

He died in 1559, a year after Elizabeth came to the throne, so in effect, he served four Tudor sovereigns. He is believed to be the only founder of an Oxbridge college to be buried under his own foundation.

W. Matthison

UNIVERSITY CHURCH

St. Mary the Virgin by Dennis Flanders

Oldest University Building

The painting Dennis Flanders has produced opposite is quintessential Oxford and one much painted by artists of every generation. In fact, this view is similar to that produced by J. M. W. Turner in 1809. It is a view of The High Street looking north. "The High" has all the classical elements of a proper street. Full of varied and handsome buildings, it curves gently and widens in the centre, giving a slightly enclosed feeling. The tree to the right, perfectly placed because it softens the somewhat stern and austere look of the buildings.

In the centre of the painting is the University Church of St. Mary the Virgin. Its richly pinnacled spire, erected about 1320, rises majestically from the somewhat plain but solid tower constructed a hundred years earlier. The body of the church was largely rebuilt in the late 15th and early 16th centuries and almost certainly stands on the site of an earlier church, dating from the foundation of Oxford as a Borough in the 9th century. In fact the original East Gate of the Borough stood on this site and St. Mary's was probably the gate church or chapel. St. Mary's was associated with the University from the late 12th century at a time when there were no specialized university buildings. It became the hub of university life and until the 18th century was the meeting place for Chancellors, Court and University Convocation. After completion of the Sheldonian Theatre in 1669 University ceremonies such as Encaenia were no longer held at St. Mary's. The weekly University sermon is the only regular institutional connection between the church and the university.

UNIVERSITY COLLEGE

The Fellows Garden by Jane Carpanini

The other Alfred legend

For many centuries "Univ" as University College is affectionately known, disputed with Balliol and Merton the distinction of being Oxford's oldest college. It is now generally accepted that Univ, founded in 1249 by William of Durham, is officially the oldest college in Oxford and, incidentally, pre-dating any Cambridge foundation.

For nearly 400 years, however, Univ had an alternative claim to superior longevity inasmuch as King Alfred was claimed to be its founder in 872. This is the second and least known Alfred legend (after the burnt cakes). There is much circumstantial evidence to support this claim, not least that Alfred was largely responsible for the restoration of learning in England after the decay in scholarship precipitated by the ravages wrought by the Vikings. Prior to this, in the 8th century at the time of Bede, England was a great seat of learning and evangelized much of Europe.

Alfred delighted in the society of learned men, such as Asser from the Monastery of St. David's in Wales and Plegmund, Archbishop of Canterbury. He planned the Anglo Saxon Chronicles but his Oxford connection was given great substance by two other learned men of this period, St. Neots a kinsman who, according to Ralph Higden's Polychronicon of 1354, helped Alfred establish public schools in Oxford. The second learned man was Grimbald who represented Alfred's greatest coup in the intellectual transfer market.

Grimbald was a scholarly monk in Flanders where he was in the service of the Archbishop of Rheims. In return for twenty fine hunting dogs Alfred obtained the services of Grimbald who, according to William Camden in 1603, founded in Oxford the Church of St. Peters in the East (now part of St. Edmund Hall) where he is reputedly buried.

Univ has relied on the Alfred connection in two successful lawsuits. One in 1380 was a serious property dispute in which Univ's lawyers invoked the protection of Richard II on the grounds that his ancestor, King Alfred, had founded the college. The second dispute in 1727 concerned the contested appointment of its Master. In the process the Court of King's Bench reaffirmed the fact of its Royal foundation by King Alfred.

In 1872 Univ unashamedly celebrated its millennium crowned by the presentation of *burnt cakes* by the Regius Professor of History. Since this date the college has been more circumspect in its allegiance to King Alfred but he is still prayed for on college feast days. What remains, however, is not only the legend, like a lot of history, but also the college's Coat of Arms, designed in the middle ages and commemorating Alfred the Great in a design taken from the coins of Edward the Confessor which, in this case, contain a cross and four martlets.

UNIVERSITY COLLEGE

High Street Front by Jane Carpanini

The last three Stuart Monarchs

Between 1634 and 1677 the college completely rebuilt itself including the addition of a battlemented gate-tower, shown in the centre of the porter's lodge and has a stone statue of Queen Anne on the street front and one of her father, James II, on the inner front.

To the left of the porter's lodge gate-tower and just on the bend in the High is a second matching castellated gate-tower, added over 100 years later from a bequest by John Radcliffe, a wealthy and successful physician whose benefactions are everywhere to be seen in Oxford. The most important of these are the Radcliffe Camera, Observatory and Infirmary. This second gate-tower leads to the eponymous Radcliffe Quadrangle which contains, on its street front, a statue of the last three Stuart monarchs on its gate-towers.

Also in Jane's painting can be seen the dome of the Shelley Memorial, under which resides a marble statue of the naked poet, Percy Bysshe Shelley, carved by Edward Onslow Ford in 1894. Shelley was an undergraduate of Univ but was expelled in 1811, after only two terms, for publishing "The Necessity of Atheism". Sadly he drowned eleven years later.

Univ can lay claim to two post war Prime Ministers, Clement Atlee, a graduate and Harold Wilson, a Fellow. Interestingly, the present Master of Univ, Lord Butler of Brockwell, served three recent Prime Ministers, Margaret Thatcher, John Major and Tony Blair - as Cabinet Secretary and Head of the Home Office Civil Service.

WADHAM COLLEGE

College Front by William Matthison

More Dined Against than Dining

Wadham was endowed in 1609 by a wealthy Devonian, Nicholas Wadham, on his deathbed. It was, however, his widow, Dorethy who, after fighting off family designs on his estate, petitioned James I for a charter. She moved with great alacrity appointing a local West Country architect, drawing up the college statutes and appointing the first Warden. This was quite an achievement for a women of 79 who directed operations from her West Country home and never once visited Oxford.

Another remarkable Wadham character was Maurice Bowra who was Warden from 1938 until his death in 1971 and was judged to be the wittiest and most flamboyant don of his generation. He was a tremendous communicator as well as being enormously learned and well read. His hospitality was lavished on not just men from his own college but to all thinking men and women throughout Oxford. Those who came under his influence included David Cecil, Isaiah Berlin, Anthony Powell, Rosamund Lehmann and Kenneth Clark. John Betjeman was moved to comment in *Summoned by the Bells* "certain then, as now, that Maurice Bowras company, taught me far more than all my tutors did". Betjaman was a Magdalen under-graduate and like many others from colleges throughout Oxford was one of those to cause Maurice Bowra to famously remark "I'm a man more dined against than dining".

Other famous Wadham men included Sir Christopher Wren and the 19th century architect, Sir Thomas Jackson, who designed the Examination Halls and Hertford's famous Bridge of Sighs. In the 20th century distinguished alumni included Poet Laureate, Cecil Day Lewis and writer and broadcaster, Melvyn Bragg.

WORCESTER COLLEGE

College Quadrangle by Dennis Roxby Bott

The Dissolution and Civil War, twice a victim

Worcester College was originally established in 1284 as Gloucester College. A house of Benedictine monks from amongst Abbeys in Gloucester, Glastonbury, Pershore and Malmesbury. Each Abbey maintained its own accommodation block or camerae, and at one time 50 or 60 Benedictine houses in the south of England were required to send students. As well as individual camerae there was a hall and chapel which all shared.

At the Dissolution in 1540 the college was closed and the chapel and library demolished. In 1560 the buildings were bought by St. John's College and re-founded as Gloucester Hall. The new establishment, however, struggled for survival and the ravages of the Civil War 1642-47 hastened its end. In 1714 Sir Thomas Cookes, a baronet of Worcestershire, was persuaded to donate £10,000 to re-found Gloucester Hall as Worcester College. The present loggia with chapel and hall, either side and library above, was started in 1720. The cottages on the north side of the quadrangle were replaced with Palladian style buildings erected between 1773-1776 to a design by Henry Keene. However, money ran out before similar buildings could be erected on the south side, which still contain the mediaeval cottage style quarters of the old Benedictine monastic college. A wonderful and picturesque contrast beloved by artists.